Wade into Grace
Transform Conflict into Personal Growth

Jozlin Parker

This book and the Attention to Formula belongs to Wade into Grace LLC. 2021

All rights reserved. No part of this book may be reproduced or used in any manner without written permission of the copyright woner except for the use of quotations in a book review. For use permission, please email info@wadeintograce.com.

Print ISBN: 978-1-7376197-0-3

Digital ISBN: 978-1-7376197-1-0

*To my wonderful husband, Chris, and my son, Micah.
Thank you for teaching me about love, life, wholeness, and grace.*

*To Brene Brown and Richard Rohr. I have never met either of you,
but I have to say, your books ruined my life. Thank you.*

*A special thank you to my editor, Natalie Frels-Busby.
This book would not have happened without you.
Thank you*

Table of Contents

Title Page..1
Introduction..3

Part One: The Attention to Intention Formula
Chapter One: Alchemy..11
Chapter Two: Step 1—Write About Variable C...........21
Chapter Three: Step 2—Box Variable B......................25
Chapter Four: Step 3—Write About Variable A..........29
Chapter Five: Step 4—Observe..................................33

Part Two: The Enneagram
Introduction..44
Type One: The Perfectionist......................................54
Type Two: The Giver..58
Type Three: The Performer......................................62
Type Four: The Romantic...66
Type Five: The Observer..70
Type Six: The Loyal Skeptic......................................74
Type Seven: The Epicure..78
Type Eight: The Protector..82
Type Nine: The Mediator...84

Conclusion..88
Resources..93

Wade into Grace

Introduction

I am fairly certain the meaning of life is to live. If you are reading this, you are alive, but are you living?

What's the difference?

Well, intentionality. Before I began using my Attention to Intention Formula, life felt like I was being pulled down a fast river, with very little control and a lot of bumps and scrapes along the way. I knew the life I wanted to live, but actually living that life felt outside of my control. Life felt like something that happened to me instead of something that was mine.

All of that changed as I developed the Formula — discovered how my own hidden intentions were wrecking my plans and learned how to manage my own expectations and life. These are all things this book will teach you how to do. But first, we need to discuss grace.

The day I finally understood grace was incomplete. A friendship I had been trying to develop had fallen apart. I was angry and could easily name all the things she did wrong, but the truth was I only blamed myself.

I was lying on the floor, crying, convinced I deserved everything that had happened with my friend when, for once, instead of thinking about the emotions I was feeling, I decided to lean in and feel the emotions I had been holding back.

I cried about a lot of things that night, but I kept returning to my friend's betrayal. After the pain turned to anger and the anger turned into acceptance, I asked myself two questions. What part of the failed friendship was my fault? What did I bring to the relationship that wasn't fair to my friend?

It was then I realized the truth. I expected too much from her. It was like our entire friendship flashed before my eyes and I could see a pattern in my behavior that had been previously hidden from me. I wanted a deeper friendship than she could give me. The pain and rejection I experienced was of my own making.

My heart broke. I lay on the floor bawling. Naming my own mistakes helped me see beyond my own pain and disappointment. I broke through the "it's all my fault" mask that kept me from seeing the truth. For the first time, I saw my own mistakes without exaggeration.

As I sat with the truth of how my behavior contributed to this conflict, something amazing happened. It was like alchemy. What began as pain and guilt transformed into a sense of peace that introduced me to grace.

I grew up hearing about grace, but I didn't really meet grace until I understood how much I needed forgiveness. Up until then, I hid behind the mask of "it is all my fault" to avoid taking responsibility for what I had done wrong. Naming what I had done wrong in the friendship allowed me to see that I had been trying to build a close friendship with someone who only wanted to use me.

Like one of those scenes in a movie where a person's life flashes before their eyes, in my mind I began to see all the little ways my behavior allowed me to be used. But instead of feeling shame and taking on all the blame, I felt guilt and recognized a pattern to my behavior.

In *Daring Greatly,* Brenè Brown defines shame as "the fear

of not being worthy of real connection."[1] Shame is debilitating, especially when you use it as an armor—a way to avoid rejection and seeing your faults.

There is not much difference between, "It is all my fault," and, "I have done nothing wrong." Both masks allow a person to escape responsibility for their behavior. Grace broke through my mask and helped me to feel guilty for what I had done wrong. The guilt was hard, but so much better than shame.

I felt peace when I acknowledged my own mistakes—my humanity—because feeling unworthy of love left me feeling irreparably broken. But my humanity felt manageable. I can learn from my mistakes. I can grow. I can figure out how to do better.

I pulled myself up and sat on the floor, still crying, but grateful for the spiritual journey. I realized I had felt led to the experience by something greater than myself. Sitting there I knew that I was coming up off that floor a changed person. It was strange to be grateful for having my mistakes in a relationship laid before me in such an undeniable way, but seeing my mistakes freed me from shame.

I was not broken, just flawed. I sat enjoying the gratitude, letting the peace fill me up, and realized that my higher power led me to recognize my mask and to see my mistakes so I could let go of shame and experience grace.

> **While my experience of grace involved a spiritual experience tied to my belief in a higher power, I do not believe a person has to be religious or spiritual to experience grace. Grace is the acknowledgement that we all make mistakes and need forgiveness and understanding from one another. It is the space we give to ourselves and others to be human. Grace is being careful to manage**

> what we expect of ourselves and others. Grace is the freedom to trust and love ourselves as we are.

After I was finished crying, I grabbed my journal and started writing about the experience. The more I wrote, the more I realized that my experience was a lot like this formula I had started using to understand my relationship with my dad. At this point, I did not know where the formula was taking me, but I knew it played a part in freeing me from shame. Naming what I had done wrong was difficult, but if that was the cost of getting rid of shame and experiencing peace, I was willing to pay it! I began to think that maybe this formula was more than I had originally thought. Maybe this was a tool to find grace?

This book is an invitation to learn to *Wade into Grace*. It is a journey into the work of changing your relationship with your past for the benefit of your future. This work has always made me feel like I was performing a type of alchemy.

Alchemists tried to change lead into gold using the Philosopher's Stone. Instead, we use the Attention to Intention Formula to change our relationship to our past so our future is free from those events. This work is often called shadow work.

Shadow Work

Shadow work is a term used to describe the process of trying to move your unconscious behavior to your conscious mind. Our unconscious behaviors exist in the shadows, unseen by us but influencing our day-to-day lives. Our Shadow Selves are not inherently negative or evil, they are just unseen. My desire for real connection and my fear of rejection were not bad, but unseen and unacknowledged, they contributed to the conflict I had with my friend.

In addition to our Shadow Self, we have our True Self and our False Self. Richard Rohr describes our False Selves as our necessary, bogus, or ego self that we need to get through ordinary life. Our False Selves are performance selves where our True Selves are who we truly are under all the insecurities and fear.[2]

My False Self believed me to be broken and unworthy of real connection. My Shadow Self contributed to the issue with an unseen belief that I could overcome rejection if I let people take advantage of me. My experience with grace helped me to see how I had contributed to the conflict by trying to be worthy enough for friendship. It let me let go of the False Self image of being broken and unworthy into a True Self understanding of my humanity.

> **The characters Te Fiti and Te Ka in Disney's Moana are wonderful examples of True Self and False Self. If you have not seen the movie, I suggest it.**

My Attention to Intention Formula helped me learn a gentle approach to shadow work. When I engage in shadow work with the Formula, I am not trying to fix myself, change myself, or even find my flaws. I am simply trying to see myself so I can understand myself.

There is a quote by Jiddu Krishamurti that says it best: "If you begin to understand what you are without trying to change it, then what you are undergoes a transformation."[3]

The main purpose of this book is to teach the Attention to Intention Formula, but you'll notice that this book isn't called "The Attention to Intention Formula." This book is called "Wade into Grace" as an invitation to engage in shadow work gently, and with grace, not shame.

If you are reading this book, you are probably hoping to find a way to understand conflict you have experienced or you want to work on personal growth. Whatever motivation led you to read this book, let yourself enter into shadow work gently, as if you were going to wade into water. Trust that this book will help you see and understand what you are.

Don't try to change it. Notice it. Understand it. And then, let grace gently perform alchemy so that "what you are undergoes a transformation."

Part 1
The Attention to Intention Formula

Chapter 1

Alchemy

When I was 12 years old, I decided I was a daddy's girl who didn't have a dad. This belief amplified the feelings of loneliness and otherness that was part of my inner landscape. When I was 16, I got on an internet message board and found my dad. At 17, I met my dad for the first time. After a DNA test proved I was, in fact, his child, I began building a relationship with the man I had only previously known through an old photograph.

Things went well at first. My dad is married and has two children. They quickly accepted me as part of the family. I loved spending time in the country, out on the porch, drinking tea, and talking with my dad. My dad's house became a haven — an escape. On one trip, my dad drove me around the land they lived on so I could learn about the property that would one day be part of my inheritance.

The words spoken to me by my dad were perfect. I was "one of the kids" and he was ready to "make up for lost time." I once spent an entire evening comforting him when he shared how terrible he felt for not being there for me as I was growing up.

Things were great, but I had concerns about the relationship. Sometimes, someone in the family would tell me my dad was upset with me. I was quick to try to understand and fix my mistakes, but it was difficult because my dad only told other people how I disappointed him and would not discuss it with me.

Any time I tried to bring up our relationship or discuss my concerns, I was dismissed and told it was all in my head. After 13 years of trying to build a relationship with my dad, it became obvious that things were not going well.

After the first few years, I was told not to expect any Christmas presents because no one was getting any this year. When I would visit, it was clear everyone but me got presents. During the annual "no one is getting presents speech," I tried to tell my dad it was okay if my siblings got presents and I did not, but he would just get mad at me.

He wanted me to pretend I was treated the same as my siblings, even when it was obvious I was not. If I didn't go along with the charade, he would get mad and yell. I got tired of how I was being treated. I set boundaries, stood up for myself, and stopped trying to earn my dad's love.

Things got a lot worse.

Out of nowhere, my dad wanted to talk about all the ways I had disappointed him. He acknowledged how distant our relationship had become, but according to him, it was my fault for being such a bad daughter.

I tried to figure out what caused this shift. He insisted nothing changed right up to the day he told me that he and his wife had sold most of their property. He dropped the "one of the kids" charade and dumped 13 years of anger and disgust on me in a few weeks.

I went from not feeling like part of the family to being told I was not part of the family. And because I was the halfsibling that just showed up, I wouldn't be given the same amount of money my siblings were getting from the sale of the property.

The abrupt change and my dad's behavior nearly broke me. I told him I would rather him keep the money and stop treating me this way. Conversations with my dad got ugly. I explained that I didn't care about the money; I just wanted to be part of the family, but he said I was nothing but a con artist.

I got desperate. I drove out to his house. I had hoped that he would stop being mean and take the time to hear what I was saying if he saw me in person. I was his daughter. Surely, he would stop hurting me long enough to listen.

I was wrong. He blamed me for our broken relationship. I begged, with tears streaming down my face, for him to see me for who I was — not the money obsessed, selfish woman he saw me as.

Somewhere in my mind, I knew I didn't deserve his contempt and anger, but that didn't stop me from joining him and blaming myself for being unlovable. I didn't want to die, but I didn't want to live as the person he convinced me I must be.

And then, everything changed.

What if I told you that you get to choose how you experience this world? What if I told you that the power to transform how you experience rejection and disappointment are within your reach?

The catch is, however, it takes hard work and practice to become skilled at taking control of how you experience this world.

The Attention to Intention Formula was born from the distress of realizing that my relationship with my dad wasn't just falling apart; it was never there to begin with. During that time, I had come across a quote in my studies:

> *"A person's identity reflects her own list of who she is*
> *but also society's list of who she is,*
> *making it the meeting place between her and society."* [4]

This quote bothered me and left me asking: If part of who I am is determined by society, then who am I? How do I become *more* of who I want to be?

As I considered the quote and my questions, I began visualizing a Venn diagram in my mind. Circle A was me, Circle B was society, and the overlapping part of the diagram, C, was my behavior when I interacted with B.

As this Venn diagram and these questions rolled around my head, I thought a lot about the situation with my dad. There were so many times when I knew what I wanted to say to him. I carefully considered my words and the tone of my voice, but at the end of the conversation, I was left wondering, "What the hell just happened?" I felt like most of my conversations with my dad were a disaster and I resented the fact that I was changing myself to try to get him to stop treating me badly.

It seemed unfair that so little of my Circle A was included in the C overlap. Why did I have to give up so much of myself to interact with others? Was life just a fight to see who could show up more? I decided that having space for A was probably something that would require more power or money than I had.

I resented the world around me for not giving space for me to just be. I also decided that there was probably something wrong with me. I probably wasn't good enough to have a dad or be allowed to be myself.

I was stuck in that way of thinking. Then I discovered another quote:

> *"Joy is not first determined by the object enjoyed as much as the prepared eye of the enjoyer."* [5]

I read it over and over and over again. It was my Venn diagram, but it was different. This quote gave me more information. I read this sentence a few times and then labeled it in my book like this:

> *"Joy,* **C**, *is not first determined by the object enjoyed,* **B**, *as much as the prepared eye of the enjoyer,* **A**.*"*

I pulled out my journal and wrote:

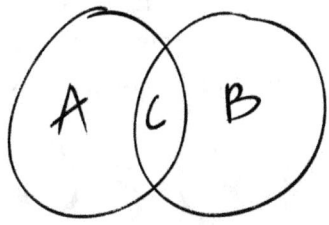

A=Me

The eye of the enjoyer

Me, you, or, the person using the Formula. Deeper than that, this variable is what I want, need, or expect out of an interaction.

CHAPTER 1

B = Object Enjoyed

Does not determine C

This could be a single person, a family, your job, an organization, or the society you live in.

C = Joy

The Outcome: What happens when A & B meet

What happened when A interacted with B? Going deeper: How did I feel? How did I react?

I realized that the three parts of my Venn diagram and the three parts of the Rohr quote were each variables in my experience of this world. I have always loved math, so using an equation made a lot of sense to me. Plus, I liked the fact that a formula allowed for A and B to affect C independent of one another. The Venn diagram made me feel like being myself was somehow dependent on the other person. Being myself didn't require the other person to be less of themselves or vice versa. We were independent variables whose interaction formed C.

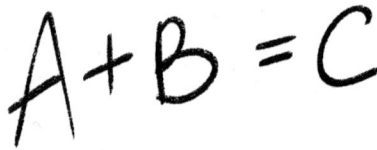

As I was letting this quote and the Formula soak in, I couldn't help but notice a few things:

First, the quote qualifies "eye of the enjoyer" by calling it *prepared*. I wasn't sure what that meant, but I *knew* I wasn't prepared. How could I prepare myself to interact with my dad?

What did that mean? Maybe there was work I needed to do in order to prepare myself so I could reach joy?

Second, I realized that part of me was ready to fight against this quote and the Formula. I knew it was important, but I also didn't like the implications. If B was not part of determining joy, then that meant finding joy was up to me. I began to feel like this quote and the Formula would require me to accept some hard truths.

Third, I wanted joy in my life, but how could I expect to have joy in my life when there were so many things outside of my control? How could I have joy in my relationship with my dad when I couldn't get him to stop treating me like he did? Maybe trying to get my dad to do what I needed him to do was the problem? It certainly wasn't helping anything!

Inner Observer vs. Inner Critic

Years of using this Formula has led me to realize what I created: a way to develop my Inner Observer.

Have you ever tried meditation? If you haven't, take a few minutes to close your eyes and try to empty your mind. If you are having trouble, try focusing on your breath.

How did it go? Did you find your mind wandering? Did you experience the voice in your head that was hard on you for not being able to focus on your breath for two minutes? That is your Inner Critic. I want to introduce you to your Inner Observer.

Every one of us has what is called an Inner Observer.

It is important to distinguish between your Inner Observer and your Inner Critic. They are not the same. An Inner Observer is a **neutral** observer to your inner life. Learning to recognize your Inner Observer is vital to the shadow work because we need it to see and understand our behavior patterns. The Inner Observer is the voice that will help move your unconscious thoughts and actions to your conscious mind without judging them as good or bad.

You and your Inner Observer have to become partners in the shadow work we are doing as we use the Attention to Intention Formula. This means you need to learn to recognize the difference between your Inner Critic and your Inner Observer.

Just being able to recognize your Inner Critic will help you recognize your Inner Observer. When you think, "That's my Inner Critic again," you are engaging with your Inner Observer. Notice how it is neutral and does not summon shame? That is the kind of personal observation and inner dialogue you need to work toward. If doing that feels impossible, that is because it is. We cannot erase our humanity; we can only give ourselves grace.

> **Naming a thing, experience, or emotion is powerful. When you can understand what you are experiencing or feeling to the point where you can put words or a name to it, a lot of your work is done. Your Inner Observer is the one who notices and names the emotions and struggles you are facing. Remember, we are simply trying to see and understand parts of ourselves. There are times it has taken me months to put a name to something. When this happens, I try to remain curious and hold that curiosity lightly. Don't go on a mental quest to name something. Let the answer come to you. Give your unconscious mind time to help. Trust that the slow, gentle path will yield a deeper understanding. With understanding comes transformation.**

The steps to use the Attention to Intention Formula are simple. What's difficult is keeping yourself from trying to force change or letting your Inner Critic rule the process. Trust yourself, your True Self, and remember to wade in gently.

The steps to use the Formula are as follows:

Step 1 – Write about Variable C

Step 2 – Box Variable B

Step 3 – Write about Variable A

Step 4 – Observe

The unnamed step in using the Attention to Intention Formula is picking a conflict or incident you want a deeper understanding of. I leave this part unnamed because once you are comfortable using the Formula with past experiences, it can also be used to prepare you for future interactions. In the next few chapters, I will discuss each step and give some helpful tips along the way.

Questions for Further Reflection:

Do you have difficulty tuning out your Inner Critic?

What are some of those intrusive thoughts that drown out your Inner Observer?

What is your relationship with shame? Can you name shame when it shows up in your thoughts?

Chapter 2

Step 1
Write About Variable C

And then, everything changed.

I thought about everything that had gone wrong in my relationship with my dad. All of the things he said, the things I said, and how much these things hurt. It was too much to put into writing, but I wrote what I could in my journal.

As I wrote, I discovered that the pain I was feeling wasn't just about the recent turmoil in my relationship with my dad, it was about our entire relationship. As I wrote, I cried. I saw how much I had denied my own fears and feelings. I saw that I wanted a dad so badly, I had let myself focus on the good parts of the relationship and deny the bad parts. I wrote for hours. I purged years of pain and confusion. This was the beginning of my journey to prepare for joy — the outcome — when A and B meet.

Writing about C, the outcome, is an important first step in Wading into Grace. We start here because it helps us to put ourselves back into the interaction we are writing about. Starting with C becomes more important as more time passes between the interaction and the present day.

While we are trying to write about a single incident, it is okay if you need to write about more than just that one incident. I needed to keep writing about my dad that day. This process is a guide. Trust yourself to know what you need and feel free to make it your own.

Getting in the zone and feeling the emotions that came up that day are important. I have found that it is helpful to approach Variable C at two levels.

Consider level one as a video camera. This level is the information that would have been captured if the interaction was filmed. This includes what happened just before the interaction, what happened during the interaction — what words were said, actions, body, language, tone of voice, etc. Don't get caught up in the small details. You're not writing a script, but you may find that remembering what color shirt someone was wearing or that it was hot outside can help you remember more. The purpose of this level is to help us remember what happened when the incident occurred so we can get to level two.

Level two is your experience of C, the incident. How did you feel? Were you happy, mad, shocked, numb? Did you feel your hands get cold? Did you feel like a rug had been pulled out from underneath you? Were you disappointed with how the conversation ended?

> **Writing about past experiences can bring up uncomfortable emotions. If you are working with a past interaction that involves trauma or writing is causing significant emotional distress, it might be helpful to reach out to a counselor or therapist for support. Some of my personal shadow work using this process had to be done with the support of a counselor. A good counselor or therapist**

> will be open to using this Formula to help you process your past interactions.

If you are writing at the camera level of C and you find yourself wanting to add in your experience, go for it! You don't have to wait and finish the camera level to start writing at the experience level. You may not need to use these two levels to write about your experience of C. If you can jump into the experience level of C, that is great. Keep these two levels as a tool you can use if you get stuck. It is also helpful to try not to worry about spelling, grammar, or the flow of your writing. It is more important to write like no one is watching than it is to follow a certain style.

> **When I used the Attention to Intention Formula, I always write with the intention to destroy or burn my writings after I am done. I need to know that what I am writing will never be seen in order to feel comfortable getting in the zone and writing Variable C. None of my work with this Formula has survived past the last step. I burn Steps 1-3 and write Step 4 in my journal so I can revisit my observations.**

Questions for Further Reflection:

Think of a time you stubbed your toe. Grab your journal and write about stubbing your toe from a video camera level. When you are finished, write about your experience of stubbing your toe. Notice the difference in how you felt writing about the two levels.

Describe a time when a conversation or situation didn't go as planned. What happened? How did you feel?

Chapter 3

Step 2
Box Variable B

"Joy is not first determined by the object enjoyed as much as the prepared eye of the enjoyer."

I stared at the quote, trying to find a way out of this next step. I knew what I needed to do, but it wasn't fair. Why should he get off so easily!

I deserved better than this. I deserve a dad. I took a deep breath and just did it. I didn't know where this formula was taking me, but I trusted the feeling I had that this was something I needed to explore. I wrote the word "dad," put a box around it, and then cried.

This is the shortest and, oftentimes, the most difficult step. After you have finished writing about C, write the name of Variable B and put a box around that name.

Why the box? Well, the box is your reminder that you cannot change Variable B. Anything inside that box is outside of your control and, honestly, none of your business. This can feel unfair, especially if the person in that box, like my dad, has an unfair negative opinion of you. Just remember, their experience of you is influenced by the stuff, Shadow Self and False Self, they brought into interactions with you. All of that is outside of your control. If you cannot control it, then it is none of your business. Treating it as your business will only cause you anxiety, pain, frustration, and suffering.

If you cannot change Variable B, and you can't, then the only way to change Variable C is to change Variable A—the only part of the equation you can change.

Once you put the box around B, you are technically finished with this step. However, there is one extra thing you can do that I have found to be a good practice.

Stop and notice how you feel about putting Variable B in the box. How does it feel to not have control over that variable? Do you accept the lack of control? Are you thinking of ways that you could possibly find a way to control or change that variable?

What Is in Your Box?

It was freeing to be able to put a box around my dad's name and declare myself free of what was outside of my control, but it didn't free me from what is inside my box. You will read this again in Chapter 4, but it cannot be said too many times: The way other people experience you is outside of your control and, therefore, none of your business. But the way you experience other people is your responsibility.

This can seem unfair, especially when the person you are interacting with is mistreating you, has authority over you, or is someone at work you can't avoid. Interacting with people whose view of you is completely different than how you see yourself is difficult, especially when their behavior is informed by their perception of you are instead of who you are. It can be so easy to justify our actions toward others based on unfair perceptions. But this lets them inform and control our actions.

At the beginning of this book, I said you can choose how you experience this world. Well, this is it right here. You choose how you experience this world by taking responsibility of your experience. This means you have to set and maintain boundaries. Boundaries are not for other people to maintain; they are for you to maintain. You have to learn to "Elsa" things that are outside of your control — just let it go!

Questions for Further Reflection:

Describe a person, group, or organization, B, you could not change. Did you realize it in the moment? How did you react?

Think about a time you tried to change something or someone you could not change.

How do you manage your experience others? Is it based on things outside of your control (the past, their experience of you, wanting that person to like you)?

If you are mistreated by someone, what are some ways you can manage how you experience that person? Would it add to the peace and grace in your life? (The answer is setting healthy boundaries.)

Chapter 4

Step 3
Write about Variable A

I was angry when I put the box around "Dad," but I was also relieved. Crying helped me move from anger to sadness and acceptance. After I cried, I moved to Variable A and started writing about what I wanted out of our relationship.

I wrote about feeling like a daddy's girl without a dad. I recognized that I carried a lot of expectations into the relationship and began asking myself if they were realistic. When I met my dad for the first time, I wanted to get to know him. I wanted to be a part of his family. All of these things seemed reasonable and, if anything, kept me from seeing the reality of my relationship with my dad until he decided to express how disappointed he was with me.

The more I wrote about what I wanted, the more I realized that it wasn't all of my fault. I said things in anger I normally wouldn't have said, but I was usually defending myself. I could have done better, but overall, I came into this relationship wanting to be part of my dad's life and family. I deserved a dad, but more than that, I didn't deserve the way he treated me.

Variable A is all about ourselves and our intentions. This is where the name Attention to Intention Formula comes from. Our goal here is to bring our intentions out of the shadows and into our conscious mind. This is not an easy task because our egos have worked to hide this information from us, but all it takes is one experience of grace-filled transformation to understand it is worth the effort.

I always start Variable A by writing about the purpose of the interaction. Some personal interactions will not have a defined purpose, but many do. Even just calling to check in is a purpose. When considering the purpose of the interaction, we are looking for our motivations, so don't stop at the easiest answer to purpose. Remember, no one will see what you write unless you let them, so ask yourself if there was more to your motivations than you care to admit.

After writing about the purpose, I consider my feelings toward the person I am interacting with. We bring our feelings about a person into every interaction we have. You don't have to write out every feeling you have about the person you are interacting with, but if you and this person experience regular conflict, it might be a good practice.

Just keep in mind, your feelings about Variable B are your business and okay to write about. But their feelings about you are none of your business. Their feelings say more about their experience of you than it says about you.

After looking at the purpose of the interaction and my feelings about the person I am interacting with, I consider what I know about myself and my behavior patterns. To do this, I use the Enneagram. Part 2 of this book is dedicated to how each Enneagram Type can use the Attention to Intention Formula.

The last thing I do for Variable A is look back at Variable C and search for keywords that could be clues for Variable A. The idea is to search for words that can help you discover what you brought into the interaction.

Be on the lookout for words like "disappointed," "frustrated," "alone," or words that convey emotions like anger or sadness. Newton's third law of physics states that every action has an equal and opposite reaction. Well, my third law of shadow work is that emotions don't just happen, they come from somewhere. Make a point to be open and curious about what you are feeling.

> **Jozlin's Four Laws of Shadow Work**
>
> 1. Shadow work must be done gently or our subconscious mind will be too afraid to allow movement into our conscious mind.
> 2. Expectations are neither good nor bad; they are either realistic or unrealistic.
> 3. Emotions don't just happen. They are data that can lead us to discover our True Selves with intentional and gentle shadow work.
> 4. The way other people experience you is none of your business. The way you experience others *is* your business.

As you write Variable A, remember that you are looking for your shadow in your actions. You are looking for opportunities to Wade into Grace by looking for where your humanity showed up in the interaction. This isn't easy, but it is worth it.

Questions for Further Reflection:

Think about a time when you felt like conflict with a person was inevitable.

How do you think that feeling impacted how you interacted with that person?

What do you think that person thinks about you? Could you be projecting your own thoughts and feelings onto the other person? What does your experience of this person tell you about yourself?

Chapter 5

Step 4
Observe

I looked over at the word "Dad" with a box around it. I thought about everything I wrote in the Variable C. I knew I couldn't change my dad, but I also knew that things couldn't keep happening the way they were between us.

Then, I experienced a wave of relief when I realized that the inability to change my dad, the box around his name, was a gift. It wasn't a loss of control or even unfair. It was freedom. I didn't have to own his rejection of me. It wasn't my fault. In fact, the way he experienced me was outside of my control and none of my business.

I looked at what I wrote for Variable A again and made an important decision. To change Variable C, I could only change A. Getting the outcome I wanted — a relationship with my dad and his family — was not something I could do by just being myself. My dad wanted me to let him treat me however he wanted and for me to pretend he was the perfect father. I realized it was not a price I was willing to pay. Just like that, the conflict was over. I was done.

I didn't say anything to my dad, I simply stopped interacting with him. I ghosted him. It took months for him to *realize that I (and, by extension his only grandchild) was no longer a part of his life. He noticed my absence when he saw my aunt had tagged me in her Facebook post wishing me a happy birthday. When he realized I had unfriended him on Facebook, he publicly disowned me in the comments of my aunt's birthday post.*

Being disowned hurt my feelings, but not like it would have before the Formula. I grieved losing what relationship I did have with my dad, but I grieved knowing I did what I could repair it.

In time, I also discovered that the distance helped me appreciate the good times in our relationship. It has been years since he disowned me. I maintain a zero-contact relationship with him, but time has brought me to a place where I can forgive him. I won't put myself in a position to be hurt by him again, but I have forgiven him.

Using the Formula, I was able to observe my relationship with my dad. Observation brought understanding. Understanding brought transformation. And finally, transformation changed my relationship with the story of my dad. For the first time, I wasn't the daddy's girl without a dad or the rejected daughter. I was someone who loved herself enough to walk away from a toxic relationship.

Observation is the final step. You have been asked to observe yourself in every step along the way, but those observations were meant to help you write more. This final observation is a bit different. This is where you want your Inner Observe to engage in this process. This step requires patience and active curiosity.

> **"Be patient toward all that is unsolved in your heart and try to love the questions themselves, like locked rooms**

> and like books that are now written in a very foreign tongue. Do not now seek the answers, which cannot be given you because you would not be able to live them. And the point is, to live everything. Live the questions now. Perhaps you will then gradually, without noticing it, live along some distant day into the answer."[6]
>
> -Rainer Maria Rilke

Start by putting your pen down. If you need to write more, you can, but there is a point when it is time to simply observe. Then, start with A and read everything you wrote. Take note of the emotions you expressed. Look at B. Review C. What did you notice in your writing? What do you feel? What do you need?

Don't be surprised if you feel like taking a walk, listening to a particular song, watching a certain movie, or reading a poem or a book. I cannot tell you how many times I have found the answer I was looking for in an activity I felt drawn to. Trust yourself and know this Formula is a journey. You may not have some life changing epiphany every time you engage your story with this Formula, but you will see yourself and that is a gift in and of itself.

The Formula in Practice:

When my son was about 7 or 8 years old, we lived close to Sea World in San Antonio. The proximity made it so we could easily go for 2-3 hours every week or two. After years of laughter-filled trips, something changed. This change made it so I dreaded taking him to Sea World. Our time in the park was still full of fun, but leaving had gotten difficult. Despite my efforts to fill most of our time at Sea World with his favorite activities, he would start crying as soon as we left the park, upset about everything we didn't get to do that day. I reduced the number of trips we took to avoid his inevitable disappointment.

I decided to use the Formula to see if I could find a solution.

$$A + B = C$$

Variable C:

When we leave Sea World, kiddo is disappointed. He cries about the things we didn't get to do while at Sea World. I remind him of all the fun things we did and I point out that he picked most of them, but nothing I do seems to make a difference. I am really disappointed because I love taking him, but I spend money and put in all this effort just to end

the day with him crying and showing zero gratitude. I don't want to stop taking him to Sea World, but I am also tired of dealing with his meltdowns.

Variable B:

Variable A:

I have begun dreading visits to Sea World. I have told the kiddo that we don't have time to do everything he would like to, but it doesn't seem to work.

It took some time to find the answer to this issue. When I did find it, I was reading "Rising Strongly" by Brène Brown[7] and her discussion of the importance of managing expectations.

I had tried to manage the kiddo's expectations by telling him we would only be there a short time, but I wondered if I had done a good enough job. What 7- to 8-year-old hears, "We can only stay for two to three hours," and really understands what that means? Maybe it wasn't his expectations that were unrealistic? Maybe the issue was my expectations?

With this new approach in hand, I planned our next trip.

I waited until we were on our way to the park before I let the kiddo know that we needed to talk about managing our expectations. We talked about only having two to three hours at Sea World, but this time, I gave him more information about what that meant.

"This means we have time for three rides and two shows. How about I pick one ride and one show and you pick the rest?"

I modeled what it looked like to manage my own expectations: "I want to see all the shows, but I know it is unrealistic to expect to see all the shows in only two or three hours, so I am going to pick the show I want to see most. I am going to pick the beluga whale show."

And, finally, throughout the day, I mentioned ways we could save time and squeeze in extra activities that fit within our two-to-three-hour window: "You know, if we skipped the orca show this trip, we could see the beluga whale show, the sea lion show, and the pet show. Is that a good trade or is seeing the orcas really important to you on this trip?"

My son never left Sea World in tears again. Managing expectations has become a regular activity in our family.

Managing Expectations:

The second law of shadow work says that expectations are neither good or bad, just realistic or unrealistic. What it doesn't say is, disappointment always points to expectations and expectations always point to our intentions. My son was disappointed he didn't get to do all he intended at Sea World and I was disappointed my son didn't comprehend my first attempt to manage his expectations the way I intended. Expectations are the clues that lead us to our subconscious intentions. This is why observing, with special attention to our expectations, is an important part of the Attention to Intention Formula.

When we are observing our relationships, it is important to take the time to examine our own expectations of ourselves and others. It could have been easy for me to ignore and resent my son's tears and punish him for his disappointment, but the Formula kept me from taking that route. Instead of trying to find a solution by controlling my son, I was forced to sit with the problem until I found a resolution.

In the end, it was me who had wrongly expected my young child to understand what I intended to communicate instead of what I actually said. How very unrealistic of me!

Preparing for Joy:

One day, I was getting ready to walk into a meeting that could lead to conflict when I noticed that I had been unconsciously using the Formula to prepare. myself

"Okay, what is the purpose of this meeting? I am nervous. I need to take some deep breaths and center myself so I can be present in the meeting and not bring in all of these negative past experiences. Man, this sucks. Well, that's another thing I am bringing with me."

Once I saw what I was doing, I began consciously using the Formula to prepare. I considered how I would word the main thing I needed to say and took out the passive aggressive qualifiers that had creeped in. Any time I started thinking about what the other person thought of me, I mentally dropped it in the "not my problem box" and smiled at the freedom I was discovering.

The meeting was terrible. I knew it would be. But I felt good knowing I had done my best. I had finally discovered how to prepare myself for joy.

Up until that meeting, the Formula was something I only intentionally used while journaling about past events. After that meeting, I regularly used the Formula to prepare myself for all meetings and most interactions. I used the behavior patterns I had recognized within myself during my shadow work with the Formula and began asking myself if I was at risk of repeating those same behaviors.

A few years after I began using this Formula, I had the opportunity to take a 10-week class about this tool called Enneagram. I knew it was a personality thing. I have always been drawn to personality tests and books, so I was excited to learn about something new.

Two weeks into the class, I was hooked. In the span of 10 weeks, I read the assigned book plus five additional Enneagram books. The knowledge and information I gained in that class and in the books I read made my shadow work with the Attention to Intention Formula even more beneficial. The Formula gave me a way to better see and understand my behavior when I interacted with others, but Enneagram put words to my Type's behavior pattern and expectations. It was invaluable.

The transformation that came from my shadow work

accelerated. Combining the Attention to Intention Formula with the Enneagram allowed me to shed even more of my Shadow Self and learn to interact with others from a place of True Self instead of False Self.

In three years, I went from suffering with severe depression, struggling with an anxiety disorder, and having random panic attacks to being described as a calming, steady presence in high-stress situations.

> **Pre-Formula Jozlin & Post-Formula Jozlin**
> Developing the Attention to Intention Formula changed my life. So much so that I feel like a different person. Pre-Formula Jozlin was so anxious and worried about what other people thought of her that she had developed an anxiety disorder. She struggled to make friends and maintain friendships. Pre-Formula Jozlin thought everything was her fault and could not figure out where she needed to grow. Post-Formula Jozlin is known as a calming presence. The first time I was described as a calming presence, I almost laughed out loud. I did not believe it. Not me, anxiety girl! After the third or fourth time of being called a calming presence, I had to keep myself from tearing up, proud of how far post-Formula Jozlin had come.

Your Turn:

Grab your journal, pick an interaction, and try out the Formula. We have included the steps below. If you feel like you might want to destroy what you write in Steps 1-3, use scratch-paper and use your journal for Step 4. Use the questions at the end of each chapter to help you with each Step.

The Attention to Intention Formula

Step 1 – Write about Variable C

Step 2 – Box Variable B

Step 3 – Write about Variable A

Step 4 – Observe

Questions for Further Reflection

How did using the Formula change the way you understood the interaction?

How much were your actions informed by how Variable B treats you?

Part 2
The Enneagram

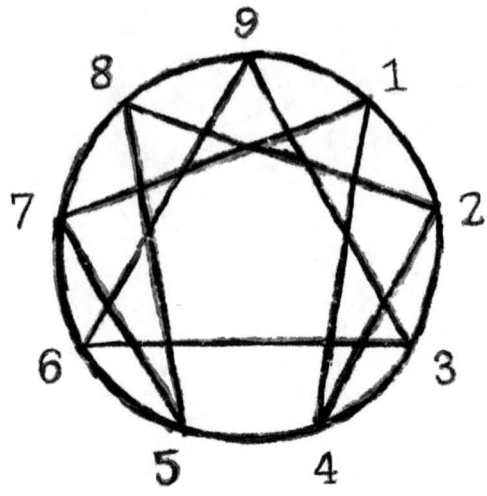

Introduction

Once upon a time, your world was free of pain and disappointment. Then, you were born. Even then, some of us came into this world having developed during a stressful pregnancy. So, it is safe to say that we have never had a time in our lives when we did not experience some form of struggle. To survive, we used coping mechanisms and developed behavior patterns.

Enneagram teaches us that our coping techniques and behavior patterns are tied to our personalities, or, more specifically, our character structures. There are nine character structures in Enneagram referred to as types.

I believe we are born with our character structures. Some Enneagram traditions teach that each type has a childhood wound and that wound is how our types are formed. There is a lot of wisdom that can be learned from these traditions, but I struggle with the implications that our personalities come from a wound we received in our childhood. Is the whole of a person's identity based on a wound? Are our personalities really the result of pain? And, if that were true, could a parent pick their child's type or keep their child from becoming a certain type by trying to manage what kind of wounds are inflicted on them?

Teaching that our types are formed during childhood or because of a childhood wound also ignores research that has recognized distinct personalities that show up in infanthood. In fact, in his article, "Nature and Nurture: on Acquiring a Type," Dr. David Daniels M.D. talks about his research on this topic. Not only have infants been found to have one of nine distinct personalities, but these nine personalities easily match up with Enneagram types.[8]

This research does not raise nature above nurture, but instead gives us an idea of how we experienced the world we were nurtured in. In his article, Daniels discusses how our types "constitute the lenses or filters with which we view or perceive the world, literally from conception not birth, what technically can be called the primary orientation bias in the way a young child views or experiences the world."

It may seem like a small distinction to make, but I feel like it is an important one, especially when we are talking about the core structure of who we are. Our personalities being the result of a childhood wound would seem to imply that we are nothing more than victims to the wounds of our childhood and slaves to the repercussions of an incident no one could prevent. The idea that our personalities were done to us means that shadow work is more about erasing ourselves instead of finding ourselves.

My personal experience with shadow work and with the Attention to Intention Formula has taught me that I experience more growth and grace when I lovingly look for my True Self in the shadows than when I try to fix and silence the little girl who wanted a dad.

Perhaps that is why my formal Enneagram education comes from the Narrative tradition. The Narrative Enneagram is a beautiful tradition that trains their teachers to meet Enneagram students where they are. Their language reflects this mission. Instead of teaching about a childhood wound, the Narrative Tradition teaches about each type's basic proposition.

Our basic proposition refers to our needs based on our character structure. This is what our type idealizes and works toward to achieve value and self-worth.

Here is a list of basic propositions by type, according to the Narrative Enneagram.[9]

Type One: You must be good and right to be worthy of love.

Type Two: You gain love and approval and fulfill your personal needs through giving to others.

Type Three: You gain love, recognition, and acceptance through performance, action, and success.

Type Four: You will feel loved, whole, and complete if you can find the ideal love or perfect circumstance.

Type Five: You can assure survival and gain protection from intrusion and insufficient resources through privacy, self-sufficiency, limiting desires, and acquiring knowledge.

Type Six: You can assure life and certainty by avoiding harm (the phobic stance) or facing it (the counter-phobic stance) through vigilance, questioning, and either battling or escaping perceived hazards.

Type Seven: You can avoid pain and frustration by inventing options, opportunities, and adventures.

Type Eight: You gain protection and respect by becoming strong and powerful, imposing your personal truth and hiding your vulnerability.

Type Nine: You gain belonging by merging with others and comfort by dispersing your energy into objects and activities.

During our life in this world, we are searching for our basic proposition and as we encounter pain and rejection, we cope. As we search for our basic propositions, we find coping techniques that protect our character structure. These coping techniques are behavior patterns called <u>defense mechanisms</u>.

Here is a list of defense mechanisms by type:

Type One: Reaction formation — feeling one thing and expressing the opposite

Type Two: Repression — suppressing "unacceptable" feelings and converting them into a more acceptable form of emotional energy

Type Three: Identification — taking on a role so completely that we lose contact with who we are inside

Type Four: Introjection — unconsciously incorporating the characteristics of a person or object into one's own psyche

Type Five: Isolation — can be physically withdrawal from others or, stay in the head and withdraw from one's emotions

Type Six: Projection — attributing inner concerns and fears to others and external situations

Type Seven: Rationalization — staying in the head, explaining away or justifying feelings and behaviors in order to avoid pain or accepting responsibility

Type Eight: Denial — the forceful redirecting of

attention and feeling based on willfulness and control
Type Nine: Narcotization — using food, drink, entertainment, or repetitive patterns of thinking and doing to "put oneself to sleep"

> **Each type has a specific defense mechanism that is their primary defense mechanism, but this does not limit a person from using defense mechanisms of other types. Because of this, it is helpful to study all nine defense mechanisms. The more you learn about defense mechanisms, the easier it will be for you to recognize them in yourself when using the Attention to Intention Formula.**

While working toward our basic propositions, our types end up developing an avoidance pattern. If your type is *looking* for harmony, it makes sense that you would *avoid* conflict. Peter O'Hanrahan's article, "The Enneagram Defense System: Access Points for Self Awareness & Growth," discusses how our idealization and basic proposition reinforces our avoidance pattern. [10] Our avoidance pattern becomes something that quietly influences our behavior and is enforced by our defense mechanism. (Sounds a bit like our Shadow Self, doesn't it?)

O'Hanrahan used the relationship between a type's basic proposition, avoidance pattern, and defense mechanism to create the defense system of each type. If you can understand your type's defense system and learn to see it in your work with the Formula, you *will* experience transformation.

Here is a list of defense systems by type:

Type Ones use reaction formation to avoid anger (i.e.

direct anger) and to maintain a self-image of being right.
Type Twos use repression of personal needs and feelings to avoid being needy and to maintain a self-image of being helpful.
Type Threes use identification to avoid failure and maintain a self-image of being successful.
Type Fours use introjection to avoid ordinariness and maintain a self-image of being authentic.
Type Fives use isolation to avoid emptiness and maintain a self-image of being knowledgeable.
Type Sixes use projection to avoid personal rejection and to maintain a self-image of being loyal.
Type Sevens use rationalization to avoid suffering and to maintain a self-image of being OK.
Type Eights use denial to avoid vulnerability and to maintain a self-image of being strong.
Type Nines use narcotization to
avoid conflict and to maintain a self-image of being comfortable or harmonious.

Wings

A distinguishing element of the Enneagram is the nine-sided figure with intersecting lines within a circle. This figure is often numbered so we can see where each Type is on the symbol. This symbol is a critical element of studying Enneagram, as it gives depth to each of the nine types and helps us to visualize and understand each Type's character structure.

Each Type's character structure includes what is called its **wing**. Every Type has two wings. A type's wings are the two types on either side of it on the Enneagram figure.

To find your wings, look at an Enneagram symbol and

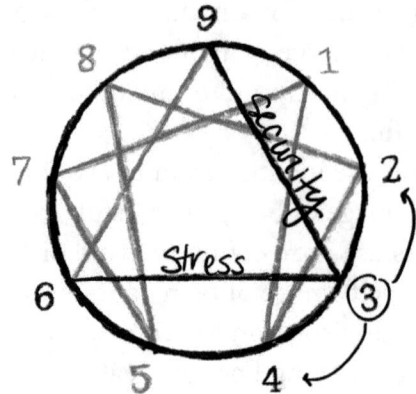

imagine drawing a circle around your type. Then draw a line to the numbers on both sides of that circle. (See example above.) The two numbers to the right and left of your number are your type's wings. Most Enneagram students find that they have a predominant wing or one wing that shows up in their character structure more than the other.

Think about your type as the foundation and shell of a house and wings as additions to your house. We come into this world with our character structure. So, our house has a foundation, wood framing, and a roof. Our floor plan and additions are based on our types and wings. As we grow up, all the details of our personality are added within the structure of our original floor plan. We can take this metaphor as far as we want, but we will leave it here for now. The idea is to begin to see how nine Enneagram character structures can be expressed in many individual ways.

Stress and Security

The intersecting lines in the Enneagram figure is one of its greatest gifts to students who study it. Each Type has two lines. One line indicates how that type moves when in stress, the other indicates how it moves in security. Another way to say it is, the lines let us know what happens when we have to reach for our basic proposition. It also delineates what happens when we feel like our basic proposition is achievable or, at least, within reach.

Our Types influence our experience of the world around us. In the Narrative Tradition, we teach that our goal is to use our knowledge of Enneagram to loosen our Type structures. Combining the study of Enneagram with the Attention to Intention Formula helps us loosen our Type structures and experience transformation through shadow work.

Let's use the story of my dad in Part 1 to take a deeper look at how a Type structure can influence a person's experience and what a loosened Type structure looks like:

As a Type 4, The Romantic, my character structure is predisposed to feeling like something is missing. Multiple types struggle with rejection, but Fours fear being rejected because they believe that something is missing or broken inside of themselves that makes them difficult/impossible to love.

Fours believe they will feel whole and complete when they can find the ideal love or circumstance. They use introjection — an unconscious habit of taking on the characteristics of a person or object as part of themselves — as a defense mechanism. This introjection can happen with positive or negative characteristics. When things go wrong in relationships, Fours tend to blame themselves.

This means that as a child, the struggles and emptiness of not having a father was amplified by my Type structure. I was predisposed to feel like something was missing. If I had grown up with my dad in my life, I would have found something else that was missing, but my Type meant I really felt and saw the lack of a father figure. And, because Type Fours tend to romanticize and idealize, I didn't just wish I had a father figure in my life, I decided that I was a daddy's girl without a dad. I made what I was missing part of my identity.

When I met my dad and his family, I wanted to be a part of his life, but I had also idealized the idea of having a dad. I wanted to meet him and have a father figure, but I was also looking for the parts of myself I believed were missing. In addition to all of this, I was afraid that my dad and his family would reject me, confirming that something was, indeed, wrong with me that made me unworthy of love. By the time I met my dad, my fear of rejection and fear that something was wrong with me had already been "confirmed" by rejection and relationship issues throughout my life. So, I honestly believed I needed to work so I could be loveable.

Fours move to Two when in stress. As I was confronted with things my dad did not like about me, I tried to help him love me by giving myself up. I stopped telling my dad how I was doing in college because he complained that I was just showing off. I went out of my way to make sure someone reminded him my birthday was coming up so he could pretend he remembered. I repressed my own feelings and needs so I could help him feel good about our relationship.

As I built up my sense of self, I loosened my Type structure. I started setting boundaries, my self-esteem grew, and I began to realize that maybe, just maybe, I was not responsible for how my dad experienced me. I could see what the right action was and act on that right action — a strength I got from a movement to Type One in security.

Using both the Enneagram and the Formula, I was able to change how I experienced the world. Instead of feeling like something was missing, I learned to see and appreciate what was there. I decided I was whole and worthy of love now, not when some perfect circumstance came along. And, most importantly, I learned how to check in with my expectations and stop blaming myself for everything that went wrong.

In the following chapters, I move type by type and list each type's wings, stress type, security type, basic proposition, defense mechanism, and defense system, as well as ways each type can apply this information to the Attention to Intention Formula. This introduction is to help you apply Enneagram to the Formula. If this is your first introduction to Enneagram, I suggest a more in-depth study.

Type One
The Perfectionist

Wings: Nine & Two
Security Type: Seven
Stress Type: Four

Basic Proposition
You must be good and right to be worthy of love.

Defense Mechanism
Reaction formation — feeling one thing and expressing the opposite.

Defense System: Ones use reaction formation to avoid anger (i.e. direct anger) and to maintain a self-image of being right.

Type Ones grew up believing they need to be good and/or right to be worthy of love. While they are called The Perfectionist, it is important to keep in mind that Ones pick the things that are important to be done perfectly. A One may have a messy house, but keep their cars cleaned and perfectly maintained. This Type has a loud and constant Inner Critic that acts as a nagging voice, constantly pointing out their mistakes and when they are wrong. When Ones turn their Inner Critic outward, they can be very opinionated and regularly criticize those around them.

Type Ones, in an attempt to be worthy of love, idealize being good and avoid anger using reaction formation. Reaction formation allows Ones to maintain the desire to do the right thing by saying they feel one way when they feel another. Ones often struggle with procrastination because the desire to do their work perfectly causes them to freeze.

Experiencing Ones: When relating to Ones, don't take their criticism personally, it is just their inner experience spilling over. In fact, Ones can be wonderful to work with because they are detail-oriented, great at planning, and not afraid to speak up and offer their opinion.

Attention to Intention Formula

Type Ones will have a harder time than most quieting their Inner Critic and learning to recognize and listen to their Inner Observer. This is due to one of the defining characteristics of a One—the ever present and ever-critical inner dialogue.

The basic proposition of a Type One is the belief that they need to be good and right to be worthy of love. When using the Formula, this type should look for times when they can recognize they were good and right, but also look for signs they may be rationalizing their behavior in order to feel right. When they do find times when they could have made a better decision, they need to remember to give themselves grace and remind themselves that they are worthy of love and grace just the way they are.

One's defense mechanism, reaction formation, will make it difficult for them to be truly honest when using the Formula. Ones' use of reaction formation will make it harder to express themselves honestly. Writing with the intention of burning or destroying their writing could help move past this defense mechanism.

Because Type One's defense system is focused on avoiding feeling like they are wrong, Ones may struggle to use The Attention to Intention Formula as it was intended. The Formula is used to help us find what we could have done better, but finding where they could have done better to a One may feel like they are looking for where they were wrong. It will be critical for Ones to approach this work gently. They need to give themselves space to be angry, to be wrong, and to still be loved.

Type One

Type Two
The Giver

Wings: One & Three
Security Type: Four
Stress Type: Eight

Basic Proposition
You gain love and approval, and fulfill your personal needs, through giving to others.

Defense Mechanism
Repression—suppressing "unacceptable" feelings and converting them into a more acceptable form of emotional energy.

Defense System: Twos use repression of personal needs and feelings to avoid being needy and to maintain a self-image of being helpful.

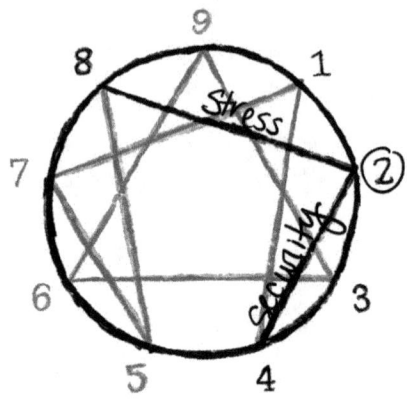

Type Twos believe they can gain love, approval, and fulfillment by giving to and helping others. The problem is, the love and approval they are looking for cannot be earned. They help and give with unrealistic expectations. No amount of gratitude or recognition from others will fulfill their need for love and approval. That need has to be met from within. Unfortunately,

Twos avoid feeling needy by repressing their own desires and giving their energy to others so they can be helpful. This defense system means that Twos have to do their shadow work so they can learn to understand and meet their own needs. When Twos don't do this work, their unrealistic expectation of finding love and approval from outside of themselves can be expressed as controlling and excessive.

Experiencing Twos: Twos are a wonderful gift to this world. They are great at jumping in and making themselves useful to a group or project. It is important to see Twos as more than just the ways they can help you or others. Because Twos repress their own needs and idealize being helpful, it is important to set, maintain, and clearly communicate boundaries.

Attention to Intention Formula

Type Twos' basic proposition is to gain love and approval through giving and helping others. However, they often give to expect more from others in return than is realistic. Their need to be needed can come across as intrusive to others. Twos will need to pay special attention to managing their expectations when helping others. They would benefit from asking themselves what they expect the person they are helping to give them in return. Or even, "How would I feel if all I got in return was a quick 'thank you?'"

Type Two's defense mechanism is repression. They repress their own needs and put their energy into helping others. Repressing your needs does not meet your needs. Those needs are still present. When using the Formula, Type Twos could ask themselves, "Is there something I need that I am trying to get from this interaction?"

Two's defense system will show up in the Formula, but they

have put effort into looking for it. This Type represses their own needs by helping others so they don't come across as needy. The problem is, they need the approval of others and when they do not get it, Twos can become intrusive and demanding. To avoid this, they will need to spend time discerning their own needs and learning how to find approval from within.

Type Three
The Performer

Wings: Two & Four
Security Type: Six
Stress Type: Nine

Basic Proposition
You gain love, recognition and acceptance through performance, action, and success.

Defense Mechanism
Identification — taking on a role so completely that we lose contact with who we are inside.

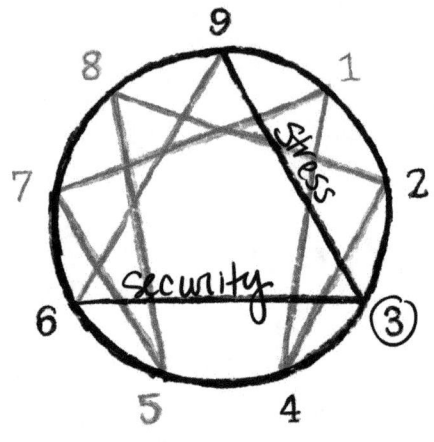

Defense System: Threes use identification to avoid failure and maintain a self-image of being successful.

Type Threes are called The Performer. While this name fits Threes, there is often a sense that this Type is dishonest in their performances. While many Threes are very open about telling small lies in order to enhance their performance and appear more successful than they feel, most Threes view these small lies as presenting the best version of the truth. This best version of the truth helps Threes gain love through performance, action, and success. Because Threes idealize success as the pathway to love, they avoid failure at all cost. Threes often say that failure isn't an option. Threes use identification as a defense mechanism to avoid failure. Their identities become completely wrapped up in the role that makes them feel successful. Threes will need to use the Formula to discover who they are outside of that role and to manage the unrealistic expectations they put on themselves.

Experiencing Threes: Threes have an incredible amount of energy and drive. They don't just get things done, they get things done at a high level of both quality and professionalism. It can be easy to fall into a trap by comparing yourself to Threes because their success and drive is difficult to ignore. Keep in mind that this drive comes from a belief that they have to hustle for love and acceptance. Their drive is part of their humanity. Do not take advantage of it. Make a point to see and even compliment Threes for who they are outside of their drive and success.

Attention to Intention Formula

Type Three's basic proposition is gaining love, recognition, and acceptance through success. They are willing to change the definition of what success is in order to feel successful. They often place unrealistic expectations on themselves. When using the Formula, Threes could have difficulty viewing the incident and discerning their own feelings during the event. It will be important for them to use the camera level of Variable C to help them dig in and find their feelings. Like Ones, Threes will struggle to see their mistakes because they avoid feeling unsuccessful. It is important that Threes remember that mistakes do not make them unsuccessful.

Threes' defense mechanism is identification. They will build their identity around the role that makes them feel successful, which makes it very difficult for Threes to see and acknowledge their identity outside of that role. Threes will need to be extra gentle with themselves as they approach working with the Formula. They will also benefit from burning or destroying their writing after they are finished.

Because Threes define what success means to them, it is possible they can make their defense system work *for* them when using the Formula. As long as they approach the work with gentle grace, Threes can reframe the work with the Formula as not looking for failures and instead decide success is finding places where they can grow, so long as they bring a level of honesty and authenticity to the process.

Type 4
The Romantic

Wings: Three & Five
Security Type: One
Stress Type: Two

Basic Proposition
You will feel loved, whole, and complete if you can find the ideal love or perfect circumstance.

Defense Mechanism
Introjection — unconsciously incorporating the characteristics of a person or object into one's own psyche.

Defense System: <u>Fours</u> use <u>introjection</u> to avoid <u>ordinariness</u> and maintain a self-image of being <u>authentic</u>.

Type Fours, The Romantic, romanticize the world around them. They believe they will feel loved and whole when they find the ideal love or perfect circumstance. They can take an ordinary situation and romanticize it into something extraordinary. While this ability can be great for creative endeavors, in everyday life, however, it means Fours have unrealistic expectations of people and experiences. Nothing will ever live up to their romanticized ideal. Fours want to be authentic and avoid being ordinary. To do this, they use introjection. Introjection happens when a person unconsciously takes on characteristics of a person or object into their own psyche. Fours romanticize the world around them, good or bad, so introjection can be positive, taking on the positive romanticized characteristics, or negative, taking on the romanticized or exaggerated blame when things go wrong. Fours will benefit from using the Formula to manage their expectations and work to see the world as it is instead of through the romantic lens they use to experience life.

Experiencing Fours: Fours are often described as having big emotions, but it is important to keep in mind that many Fours feel like the emotions they express are small compared to what they feel. Fours do not shy away from feeling the depths of sadness and pain. They enjoy deep conversations and can be great listeners. It is important to keep in mind that Fours often fall into the habit of expecting too much from people and situations. Don't take it personally if reality falls short of their expectations, as it often does.

Attention to Intention Formula

Type Four's basic proposition is that they will feel loved and whole when they find the ideal love or circumstance. This desire to find what they consider to be the ideal can cause them to have unrealistic expectations on the people and circumstances. When you are looking for the magical in the mundane, you will be disappointed. Fours will need to develop a practice of managing their expectations and finding the beauty in everyday life.

Fours' defense mechanism is introjection. Introjection can be positive — idealizing others — or negative — shaming self. Both expressions of introjection lead Fours to have unrealistic expectations. Fours will need to learn to notice this defense mechanism so they can maintain their own identity and learn to recognize their unrealistic expectations.

Fours want to be authentic, but work to avoid feeling ordinary. Their defense mechanism causes them to expect more from life than is available, even when their life is quite extraordinary. Their continuous reaching for what is missing can cause them to abandon themselves. Fours need to learn to use the Formula so they can recognize this behavior pattern, avoid losing themselves, and find true authenticity.

Type 5
The Observer

Wings: Four & Six
Security Type: Eight
Stress Type: Seven

Basic Proposition
You can assure survival and gain protection from intrusion and insufficient resources through privacy, self-sufficiency, limiting desires, and acquiring knowledge.

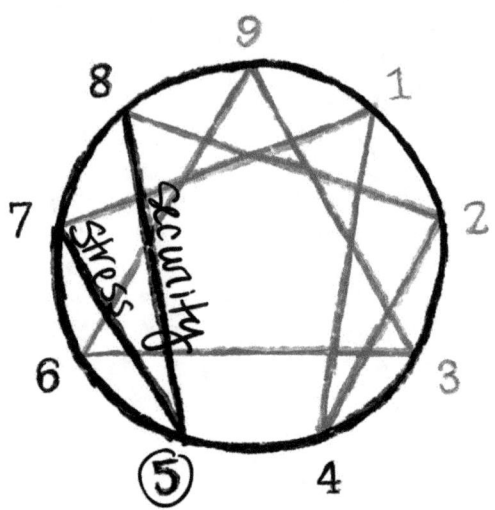

Defense Mechanism
Isolation — can be physically withdrawal from others or stay in the head and withdraw from one's emotions.

Defense System: <u>Fives</u> use <u>isolation</u> to avoid <u>emptiness</u> and maintain a self-image of being <u>knowledgeable</u>.

Type Fives believe they can survive and protect themselves from intrusion and insufficient resources through privacy, self-sufficiency, and acquiring knowledge. A word often used to describe Fives is "selfish," but for the purpose of this book and utilizing the Attention to Intention Formula, I would describe

Fives as being quick to judge other people's expectations of their time and resources as unrealistic. Fives use resources, particularly their knowledge, to feel safe and secure. Fives idealize their resources and use isolation to avoid feeling empty. Fives have a habit of keeping their knowledge to themselves, feeling as though they can never acquire enough to be secure in sharing what they know. This comes from a fear of their knowledge being incomplete or being seen as incompetent and thus, shattering their idealized identity of being knowledgeable. Fives seek out knowledge about themselves and the world around them, so will likely see the Attention to Intention Formula as a tool they can use to gain more knowledge. Fives will have to work to not keep what they learn from using the Formula to themselves and put it into practice.

Experiencing Fives: The Observer is a great name for this Type. In group settings, Fives often listen before they speak and many are pleased if they avoid speaking in front of the group at all. If a Five is in your group, don't assume they have nothing to say if they don't speak up. In fact, Fives that feel safe sharing their knowledge add a great deal to the group. Invite Fives to share, but do not rush them. Fives often pause before or while they speak. Be patient. It will be worth it.

Attention to Intention Formula

Type Five's basic proposition is that they will survive through privacy, being self-sufficient, and acquiring knowledge. A word often associated with them is stingy. Because of this, Fives will benefit from learning how prone they are to deciding someone else is expecting too much from them. Out of all the types, Fives are the most likely to believe that realistic expectations from others are unrealistic. Fives need to acknowledge their own need to hoard time, resources, and knowledge so they can recognize when it comes up in their relationships.

Fives' defense mechanism is isolation. They will need to look at their interactions with others and learn to see where the need to isolate was the primary motivating force behind decisions. Isolation in and of itself is not a bad thing, but Fives will want to look to make sure their isolation is not taking over their lives. Not all isolation happens alone. Fives will need to ask themselves if they were present during an incident or just there when it happened.

Fives isolate to avoid feeling empty and to appear knowledgeable. The problem with this defense system is that knowledge is not going to satisfy the emptiness they feel. Relationships, on the other hand, can help fill that emptiness. Fives need to use the Formula to help them discover the right balance of isolation and socialization. Fives often have a wealth of information. They have a difficult time sharing their knowledge because they expect themselves to be a top expert before they will share information with others. Because of this, Fives would benefit from asking themselves if they are expecting too much of themselves before they feel comfortable sharing.

Type Five

Type 6
The Loyal Skeptic

Wings: Five & Seven
Security Type: Nine
Stress Type: Three

Basic Proposition
You can assure life and certainty by avoiding harm (the phobic stance) or facing it (the counter-phobic stance) through vigilance, questioning, and either battling or escaping perceived hazards.

Defense Mechanism
Projection — attributing inner concerns and fears to others and external situations.

Defense System: <u>Sixes</u> use <u>projection</u> to avoid <u>personal rejection</u> and to maintain a self-image of being <u>loyal</u>.

Type Sixes have two stances. A Six's stance tells us their position when responding to fear. The phobic stance assures life and certainty through vigilance, avoiding harm, questioning, and escaping perceived harms. The counter-phobic stance assures life and certainty through vigilance, facing harm, questioning, and battling perceived harms. Sixes often favor one stance over the other, but can switch stances when situations or roles change. Both stances are searching for certainty and often make decisions by polling family, friends, or co-workers. Sixes idealize loyalty and try to avoid personal rejection using the defense mechanism projection. Projection is when a person takes their personal feelings and concerns and projects them on the world around them. Oftentimes, this projection shapes how a Six experiences the world around them, overriding evidence that reality is not based on their feelings.

Experiencing Sixes: Sixes are great at finding potential issues or flaws in preparations and planning. This can be a wonderful asset, but can become difficult when a Six does not know how to manage their concerns. It is important to keep in mind that the concerns of a Six feel very real to them. Don't take their concerns personally. Sixes' use of projection can cause them to form opinions about people and situations that are based on their feelings instead of reality. Don't take it personally if a Six accuses you of something based on their fears and concerns of their inner world. Remember, that is their responsibility, not yours.

Attention to Intention Formula

Type Six's basic proposition is that they can obtain certainty by avoiding harm or through being vigilant, questioning, or battling perceived hazards. When using the Formula, they will need to be aware of their tendency to be on the lookout for danger or disloyalty. Not every mistake someone makes is a sign of disloyalty or harmful intentions.

Sixes' defense mechanism, projection, can be a useful tool in personal growth. Projection works as a mirror. If a Six can recognize their own concerns and then use that concern to look back inside themselves, they can turn their defense mechanism into a way to see growth opportunities.

This Type's defense system is to use projection in order to avoid personal rejection so they can seem loyal. The problem is that Sixes often believe their projections are an accurate reflection of reality. Their attempts to avoid personal rejection often cause the situations that lead them to be rejected. If Sixes can learn to use the Formula to recognize their tendency to project before it disrupts their relationships, then they can have longer lasting, loyal relationships.

TYPE SIX

Type Seven
The Epicure

Wings: Six & Eight
Security Type: Five
Stress Type: One

Basic Proposition
You can avoid pain and frustration by inventing options, opportunities, and adventures.

Defense Mechanism
Rationalization — staying in the head or explaining away or justifying feelings and behaviors in order to avoid pain or accepting responsibility.

Defense System: <u>Sevens</u> use <u>rationalization</u> to avoid <u>suffering</u> and to maintain a self-image of being <u>okay</u>.

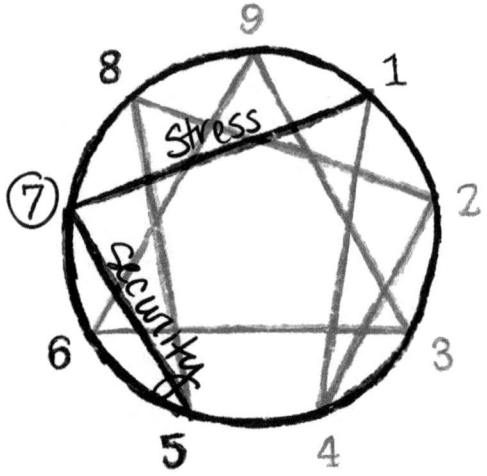

Type Sevens seek out and invent options, opportunities, and adventures so they can avoid pain and frustration. Sevens are often described as having trouble focusing because they tend to jump from one task to the next to avoid boredom or escape frustration. Most Sevens come across as outgoing, active, and fairly easygoing, but their focus on avoiding suffering and trying new things can lead Sevens to struggle with varying forms of addiction. Sevens idealize being okay and use rationalization to justify moving from one thing to the next thing. When Sevens are focused on a project or task, they know how to bring lighthearted fun into the group.

Experiencing Sevens: Sevens can be a joy to experience. When a Seven doesn't make it to a meeting or gathering, their absence is noticed because of the energy they bring with their presence. Sevens who have trouble focusing their energy can be challenging to work with when they are approaching deadlines or when the work gets frustrating or boring. They are usually not people who care to do detailed, repetitive work. Don't be surprised when a Seven comes up with ways they can use their strengths or make their work more fun. It is often worth giving them this grace.

Attention to Intention Formula

Type Seven's basic proposition is to avoid pain by inventing options, opportunities, and adventure. The problem is, avoiding pain can also cause us to avoid joy as well. Sevens can use the Formula to identify the pain they are missing out on. It will seem counterintuitive to a seven to work to feel negative emotions, but they have to learn to feel so they can experience the joy of pain being transformed.

A Seven's defense mechanism is rationalization. The difference between rationalization and being rational is subtle, but important. When we are rational, we look at the evidence and form a conclusion. When we are rationalizing, we form a conclusion and then look for evidence. Sevens will benefit in using the Formula to discern when they are rationalizing something that could cause them pain or frustration.

Type Seven's defense system is to use rationalization to avoid pain and suffering so they can be okay. Sevens have to constantly work to maintain that sense of being okay, especially during times of stress and struggle. Sevens can use the Formula to learn about the behaviors they use to feel okay. Out of all the types, Sevens are the most likely to expect the least from other people so they can avoid feeling the pain of disappointment.

Type Eight
The Protector

Wings: Seven & Nine
Security Type: Two
Stress Type: Five

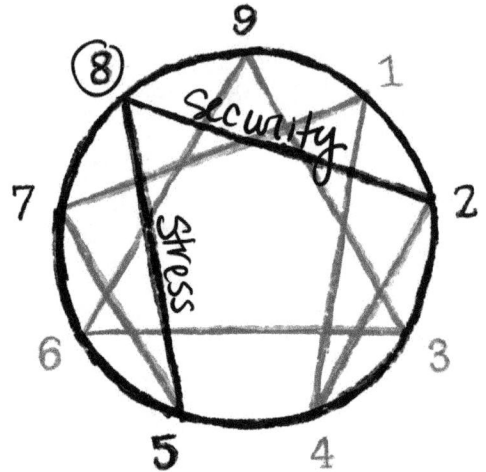

Basic Proposition
You gain protection and respect by becoming strong and powerful, imposing your personal truth and hiding your vulnerability.

Defense Mechanism
Denial — the forceful redirecting of attention and feeling based on willfulness and control.

Defense System: Eights use denial to avoid vulnerability and to maintain a self-image of being strong.

Type Eights believe that you gain protection and respect by being strong and powerful. Their strength and power are often expressed by imposing their personal truth on others and hiding their vulnerability. They idealize being strong and use denial to avoid vulnerability. Eights often hear that they are "too much" or that they come on too strong. They are people who enjoy a healthy debate, they are decisive, and they are not afraid to speak up. Eights sometimes forget that what they see as right and true is not always right and true for others. Some Eights are quick to lose their tempers, raise their voice, or express their growing frustration.

Experiencing Eights: Eights are often seen as difficult and, truthfully, they can be, but I have also found that Eight's gifts are well worth the grace you give. It is helpful to learn not to take it personally if an Eight raises their voice, is curt, or argues their point passionately.

Attention to Intention Formula

Type Eight's basic proposition is to gain protection by being strong and powerful. Unfortunately, they often find that their strength and power come at the cost of those around them. Eights often forget that they are not the holders of truth. They will benefit from using the Formula to discover when they have used their strength and power at the cost of others. It is unrealistic to expect everyone else's truth to match their own. The better they are at recognizing this tendency, the less Eights will be perceived as overpowering.

Eights use denial to redirect their attention and feelings. The good news is that the Formula was designed to combat denial by bringing our subconscious shadow selves into our conscious attention. It will be important for Eights to see and acknowledge the strength required to do deep shadow work.

This Type's defense system is to use denial to avoid vulnerability so they feel strong; however, it takes strength to be vulnerable. Eights will need to practice vulnerability. The Formula will help them discern safe and appropriate times to show their vulnerability.

Type Nine
The Mediator

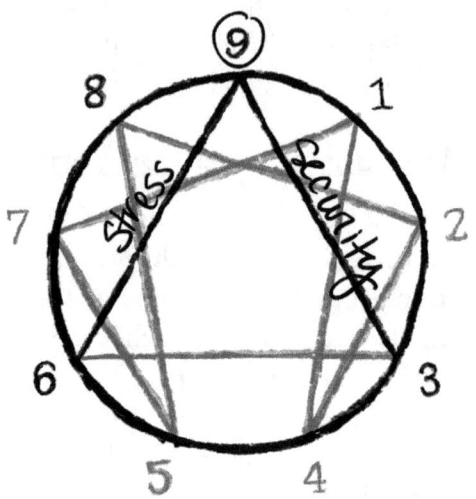

Wings: Eight & One
Security Type: Three
Stress Type: Six

Basic Proposition
You gain belonging by merging with others and comfort by dispersing your energy into objects and activities.

Defense Mechanism
Narcotization — using food, drink, entertainment, or repetitive patterns of thinking and doing to "put oneself to sleep."

Defense System: Nines use narcotization to avoid conflict and to maintain a self-image of being comfortable or harmonious.

Type Nines gain belonging by merging with others and comfort by putting their energy into objects and activities. Nines merge with others through self-forgetting and going with the flow. They avoid conflict through the use of narcotization to achieve their ideal state of being comfortable or harmonious. Narcotization — what we do when we "Netflix and chill," for example — is a defense mechanism used by all types, but Nines take narcotization to the next level. Nines can be very productive and still lose themselves in repetitive tasks. Their ability to check out helps them feel comfortable in the moment, but it comes with a cost. Nines are known for being stubborn and passive aggressive. Their conscious mind self-forgets, but their subconscious mind doesn't. Nines can have trouble noticing when they get angry, but have an easier time recognizing that they get frustrated.

Experiencing Nines: Nines are a very easy type to experience. While they can be stubborn and passive aggressive at times, most of the time they are easygoing, helpful, and agreeable. It is important to manage your expectations of Nines. Remember, their desire to avoid conflict makes it difficult for them to say no. If you get the sense that a Nine may not want to help, extend them grace by giving them an easy out and see if they take it. If you mistreat or take advantage of a Nine, you will discover just how stubborn, passive aggressive, and immovable they can be.

Attention to Intention Formula

Type Nine's basic proposition is to gain belonging by merging with others and to find comfort by losing themselves in objects and activities. They will benefit from using the Formula to help determine why they are doing something. Nines are great at seeing and supporting the needs of others, but struggle to identify their own needs. This can lead to passive aggressive behaviors. Nines can use the Formula to dig into their passive aggressive actions and work to discover the unmet needs underneath.

Nines use narcotization to escape and move through life on autopilot. They will benefit from asking themselves what they get through repetitive actions or behaviors. All types narcotize. It can be a good way to escape and recharge, but Nines need to find a balance in their tendency to narcotize. They can use the Formula to discover what their needs are so they do not feel the need to narcotize as often.

This Type narcotizes to avoid conflict so they can feel comfortable and harmonious. When Nines merge their identities with others and self-forget, they give up the chance to belong as themselves. Nines can use the Formula to understand when they are merging with others and when they are being themselves.

Type Nine

Conclusion

I have one more story to tell.

I was 21 years old, sitting in my car in the Wal-Mart parking lot, trying to gather up the energy it would take for me to go inside. At this point in my life, just being out in public was difficult. I was depressed, dealing with a lot of anxiety, and being around people required me to interact with a world I was trying to escape.

A woman walked by the front of my car and I mentally criticized everything about her. And while she never heard any of the ugly comments that were going through my head, I felt guilty for the way I had treated her.

"Wow, that was terrible. I really shouldn't be like that."

"So much for loving your neighbor as yourself. I am a terrible person."

"Love my neighbor as myself. Well, there is the problem, I don't love myself."

"Geez. I mean, clearly I don't like myself, but I didn't realize I don't even love myself. Crap."

"Why would I love myself?"

"How can I love myself?"

"I want to, but I don't know how to get there from here."

"I wonder. If I can use my love of myself to help me love my neighbor, could I love my neighbor and learn to love myself?"

I took a deep breath and got out of my car. I have always seen myself as a smart, logical type of person, so I decided to run a little experiment on myself. If my ugly thoughts toward that woman was the product of how I saw myself, then maybe I could influence how I saw myself by changing how I saw others. I set myself a measurable goal and thought through the parameters of my experiment. If I had written up my experiment, it would have looked something like this:

Problem: I do not love myself. I probably should.

Hypothesis: If there is a relationship between how I see myself and how I see others, changing one could affect the other.

Procedure: As I encounter people, I am going to mentally find one good thing about everyone I see.

Data: Each time I step in front of a mirror, I am going to be mindful of how I react to seeing myself.

The results of my experiment made an immediate impact on my life. First, it was simple things. When I got back to the car, I realized that I had enjoyed my time in Wal-Mart. From then on, going to the store wasn't something I dreaded as much as I used to. Then, I noticed that people smiled at me more and I discovered that I was smiling without having to think about it, much less force it.

One day, I felt compelled to stop and compliment a perfect stranger. It was a wonderful experience. The woman teared up a little and told me how much she needed to hear that she was still beautiful. The changes I experienced far exceeded anything I had anticipated, so I wasn't surprised the first time I stepped in front of the mirror, looked at myself, and smiled.

Do you see what I was doing during my experiment? I hope you do because it is the point of this entire book. I set an *intention* and kept it active in my *attention*. By doing that, I overwrote the intentions that were outside of my attention. Doing this changed how I experienced the world and, over time, myself.

Forgive the comparison, but a wonderful example of this is seen in dog training. Doorbell rings, dog barks. There are two approaches to stopping this behavior. You can try to stop the behavior by telling the dog "no" or punishing it for barking. Or you can overwrite the barking by teaching the dog to sit quietly in its bed when the doorbell rings. Which approach do you think would have the most success?

What does this have to do with the Attention to Intention Formula and Enneagram? Everything! Enneagram names our behavior patterns so we can understand how our character structure influences our behavior. The Formula helps us understand conflict we have had in the past by identifying what we bring into our interactions and prepares us for future interactions.

Together, these two tools help us to discover our Shadow Intentions — the subconscious intentions that come from our Shadow or False Selves and shape our expectations. These Shadow Intentions are much like what happens when a doorbell rings and a dog barks. With no instruction on what to do when the doorbell rings, a dog's instincts and nature take over.

At the beginning of this book, I said the difference between being alive and living was intentionality. Most of this book has been about how to use the Formula and Enneagram to identify Shadow Intentions by analyzing past interactions, searching for behavior patterns, and using our Enneagram Type. That is why the Formula is called the Attention to Intention Formula; it helps bring *attention* to our hidden *intentions*.

That work in and of itself is difficult. It has left me curled up in a ball on a pile of dirty clothes at the bottom of my closet, crying over mistakes I made that I couldn't see until then. It's worth it, but the end goal isn't just to see our Shadow Intentions; our goal is to live our life with intention. We need to put our *attention* on new *intentions*.

The Formula helps you bring *attention* to hidden *intentions* so you can change your relationship with your past and let go of behavior patterns that influence how you experience the world. This work makes it easier for us to keep our *attention* on the *intention* we want for our life. You don't have to pick just one intention and you don't have to use the Formula before you set new intentions. With that in mind, I would like to suggest an intention for you to set for your life right now. Grace.

In the introduction, I gave a few definitions of grace, but my favorite was the last one: Grace is the freedom to trust and love ourselves as we are. The 21-year-old version of me could not have become who I am today without the grace I gave myself back then. You cannot become who you are working toward becoming unless you give yourself grace.

Grace is an intention that gives you space to love yourself while also acknowledging your humanity — that you will make mistakes. We cannot undo our humanity, but we can love ourselves. We can grow. We can decide how we experience our life. We can Wade into Grace.

Resources

NarrativeEnneagram.org

The Narrative Enneagram was founded by Helen Palmer and David Daniels. It is a non-proft organization dedicated to Enneagram education. The type names and descriptions come from the Narrative Enneagram website. You can find a type test on their website or you can reach out to one of their certified Narrative Enneagram teachers. Narrative Enneagram teachers can be found all over the world. Many will offer Typing Interviews where they will help you narrow down your Enneagram type. If you are interested in becoming a Narrative Enneagram Teacher, their training program is wonderful.

WadeIntoGrace.com

Check out the Wade into Grace website for more information about using the Attention to Intention Formula and ways to learn how to *Wade into Grace*. If you are looking for support as you learn to apply the Formula to your life, you can book coaching sessions with a Wade into Grace coach or Jozlin. If would like to schedule Jozlin to speak at your event, email info@wadeintograce.com.

Wade into Grace Podcast

The Wade into Grace Podcast is a great way to get support on your journey to *Wade into Grace*. Episodes are either Affirmation, Meditations, Teachings, or Interviews. You can find the Wade into Grace Podcast on your favorite podcasting platform.

BIBLIOGRAPHY

1. Brown, Brene. Daring Greatly: How the Courage to Be Vulnerable Transforms the Way We Live, Love, Parent, and Lead. Penguin Random House Audio Publishing Group, 2017.

2. Rohr, Richard. Immortal Diamond: the Search for Our True Self. Jossey-Bass, 2013.

3. Jiddu Krishnamurti Quotes. (n.d.). BrainyQuote.com. Retrieved July 17, 2021, from BrainyQuote.com Web site: https://www.brainyquote.com/quotes/jiddu_krishnamurti_752641

4. Markus, Hazel Rose. Race, Gender, Sexuality, and Social Class: Dimensions of Inequality and Identity, edited by Susan J. Ferguson, SAGE, 2016, pp. 179–188.

5. Rohr, Richard, and Mike Morrell. The Divine Dance: the Trinity and Your Transformation. Whitaker House, 2020.

6. Rilke, Rainer Maria, et al. Letters to a Young Poet. Random House, 1984.

7. Brown Brené. Rising Strong: How the Ability to Reset Transforms the Way We Live, Love, Parent, and Lead. Random House, 2017.

8. Daniels, David. "Nature AND Nurture: Acquiring an Enneagram Type." David N. Daniels, M.D., 5 June 2020, drdaviddaniels.com/articles/nature-and-nurture/.

9. various. (n.d.). Enneagram Worldwide. The Narrative Enneagram. https://www.narrativeenneagram.org/.

10. O'Hanrahan, P. (n.d.). Defense Systems. THE ENNEAGRAM AT WORK. https://theenneagramatwork.com/defense-systems.

WADE INTO GRACE

www.ingramcontent.com/pod-product-compliance
Lightning Source LLC
LaVergne TN
LVHW051526070426
835507LV00023B/3335